A NEW APPROACH TO BUDDHISM

CONCERNING THE AUTHOR

Dhiravamsa is at present a meditation master at Valley Meditation Centre, Lynton, Devon, England. From 1966 to 1970, he served as the chief incumbent monk at the Buddhapadipa Temple, London. From September 7, 1968 until January 7, 1973, he was concurrently meditation master at the Vipassana Centre, Hindhead, Surrey. Besides the present work he is also the author of *The Real Way to Awakening* and *The Middle Path of Life.*

The author's interest in meditation began early in his monastic life in a small village temple in northeastern Thailand where he was ordained as a novice *(sāmanera)* at the age of thirteen. He then began to meditate under the guidance of an elderly monk. When he was eighteen Dhiravamsa moved to Bangkok where he studied and practiced Buddhism both at traditional monastic schools and at Mahachulalongkorn Buddhist University. It was during his studies at this University that he engaged more seriously in the practice of both *samatha* and *vipassana* forms of meditation. The former aims at the attainment of mental trance or absorption while the latter focuses on "insight into things as they really are." It was *vipassana* which attracted Dhiravamsa most and he still sees this as the means for realizing the truth.

Dhiravamsa has lectured and taught meditation extensively in England, on the Continent and in North America. He first visited the United States in January, 1969, when he conducted a meditation workshop at Oberlin College and lectured at several colleges and universities. Since then he has returned to Canada and to the States annually for periods of two to five months, invited by many universities and colleges including Swarthmore, Colgate, Amherst, Haverford, University of Pennsylvania, Princeton, Earlham, Carleton, Middlebury and Florida State.

In October, 1971, Dhiravamsa gave up the robe after twenty-three years as a Buddhist monk. Now he leads a meditative life, continuing his work of teaching meditation and other related activities.

DHIRAVAMSA

a new approach to buddhism

to

buddhism

by dhiravamsa

**THE
DAWN HORSE PRESS**
•LOWER LAKE, CALIFORNIA•

First Edition, 1972
This Dawn Horse Press Edition published 1974
Second printing 1978
International Standard Book Number 0-913922-08-0
Library of Congress Catalogue Card Number 74-81623

Published by
The Dawn Horse Press
Star Route 2
Middletown, California 95461

Printed in the United States of America

CONTENTS

INTRODUCTION

THIS SERIES OF LECTURES will concern a new approach to Buddhism. First of all, let us be clear what we mean by a new approach and its scope, so that we shall not carry confusion with us in treading upon the Buddha's Middle Path, which is the way of balance in the views and practice of life.

As you will have noticed, there are many approaches to Buddhism, both in the East and here in the West, depending upon the temperaments, attitudes, culture and level of knowledge of different people. As a result, there are various schools and sects in Buddhism which tend to divide people into different categories and compartments, creating conflict and bringing about disharmony. Also, the true teaching of the Buddha is frequently obscured or distorted by ideas, speculation, traditions and beliefs. There is a gap between the practice of life and the ideals of religious teachings, and this gap will never be filled by a narrow perception of the real meaning which lies behind religion.

For this reason, a new approach is being introduced to enable people to have a clearer insight into the subject of the Buddha-Dhamma. In order to see anything in a fresh way, we need to leave aside dogmatic assertions, traditions, beliefs, and even knowledge and information concerning Buddhism. Otherwise, we shall not see things anew but remain tied to a kind of repetition in which there is boredom, conflict, contradiction, and a form of sleep. Instead, we need the way of awakening, being alert, aware and sensitive to all aspects of life through a constant movement of attention and observation, in which there is no preconceived idea.

When action in life is practised in the spirit of bare attention and objective awareness, intuitive insight will flow into all activities. In this way, man can become spontaneous, natural and free in whatever he does. If we observe ourselves we shall see the reason why this spontaneity has been lost. It is because we are conformists, being restricted by what we have been taught

5

or by experiences to which we have been exposed since we were born, holding us to certain patterns of behaviour and systems of thought. Therefore we are so heavily burdened that we cannot let life flow.

We are thus enquiring into the possibility of having a new dimension in our attitude to life as a living reality, in which everything is integrated because it is understood. This requires freedom from attachment to the dogmas of organised religion, and the renunciation of the self, so that in our journey through life we shall not be diverted by ego-trips, or by ego plans for becoming something or somebody.

LIFE AND DEATH

LIFE AND DEATH is the subject of our discussion this evening, but we are not going to talk about the theory of life or the theory of death. We should investigate this subject through our experience and our own insight into what life and death mean. While I am talking do not think about principles based on what is said, written, or believed, as this would make it an already dry subject.

Throughout all ages, we human beings have looked for the meaning of life, the meaning of being, the meaning of living on Earth—why we are born into this life, why we come to this world, what is our destination, what is the end of life. Some may think that the end of life is death, and after death it will not matter what happens. Some people care about death; and some are very afraid of it, not wanting to talk about it because this increases their fear. And what may be more important is that many people are afraid of life, of living. This is because we do not really know what will happen if we lower our defences, if we allow life to give anything it has and experience it without relying upon previous knowledge. We should bear this in mind as we gradually explore what life and death really are.

When thinking 'realistically', our concepts are always dualistic: life and death, truth and falsehood, body and mind, and so on. This dualism arises through the thinking mind. We should discover whether such concepts are completely separate from each other. Is life quite different from death, or death completely distinct from life?

If you pick up a dead leaf and hold it in the sun, looking at it without having any concept about it as to whether it is dead or living, seeing it with a quiet mind free from knowledge or attitudes, observing it silently and deeply, there is the perception of life. There is a kind of living energy moving gently in that looking.

It is not actually moving in the dead leaf, but we see that what we call dead is not really dead. Although the dead leaf is limited, we can see vitality in it because it is a part of life. We cannot therefore separate life from the dead leaf. Similarly, if you go to the sea and see its wildness, watching what is going on in the water, the waves, the bubbles, the movement, sometimes violent and sometimes gentle, you will perceive life.

Sometimes when we are sitting quietly in a room, in a car, a bus, a train, and we come into contact with something in the depths of our being, we have the feeling of life, of being. Perhaps if we go deeply enough into this we may be able to die to all memories, to all thought. To live for an instant we may have a kind of experience of death, and that death is a living reality—it is called the Deathless. It never dies because it was never born. Anything born into life, into form, is subject to death, to decay.

We may say that there is conventional death and ultimate death. (We have to use some intellect in this case in order to grasp something deeper or beyond what we know already.) What is conventional death? We mean the non-functioning of something. When somebody dies we see that body ceasing to function as a 'person'. We can also refer to somebody as being 'dead' when we mean he has no liveliness or no sensitivity. Such a person appears to have no creativity, no future. There may be many more people than we realise who are dead in this way—who are insensitive and lack awareness of what is really going on within themselves and outside. The senses become dull and do not operate properly, and within the mind there is the feeling of dryness, of heaviness, which are the signs of death. This kind of death is a non-creative state, something negative and unproductive.

What is the meaning of ultimate death? In Buddhism, this refers to the Deathless, which is no different from true living because it is Being without Becoming. This does not mean something static, unmoving. It moves very gently and smoothly in the depths of our being. It does not move in the ordinary sense of movement but in the sense of being, a living reality. A living thing may move without our being able to perceive its motion, but if we develop the power of awareness we shall perceive the movement of life, uninterrupted by external movements. Why can we not see it usually? This is because of the clouding or distraction of the mind by things which claim its attention. We are thus prevented from looking into the depths of the movement of life.

Actually, the deep movement of life is very ordinary in the way it works, because it has no complexity. It moves without any preconceived ideas of where it should go, but with the clarity of understanding its own way. An idea or a destination is not required for such movement because within it there is insight—it lacks nothing. But in conventional life we always have ideas, a purpose, a reason, for everything we do. This restricts us in doing things in the way they should be done, because our aims narrow the mind to a point and wider perception is excluded. We do not look, so we do not know. That is why the Buddha said that perception could be distorted when it becomes a narrow process of perceiving. When perception is broad it ceases to be perception in the conventional sense, and can become a total perception of reality which is complete awareness of what is going on.

When we perceive the movement of life we may have a feeling of happiness, peace, and well-being, in which superficial things have calmed down so they do not disturb us. The brain can then rest so that it will work properly in dealing with life. What prevents us from seeing the movement of life is the cloud of thought, the thinking mind. We are afraid to stop thinking because we may feel we cannot be human beings without thought, or we may die if the mind stops thinking. Again, the fear of death arises, without understanding what life is. It is the ego which is afraid of dying. It must try its best to exist and maintain its own progress. Ego always has an aim, a purpose for doing things, and overlooks the actual action, the activities which should be carried out properly.

How does life come to be? Who creates life for us? All religions try to give the answer to this. We may attribute creation to something unknown, powerful and supreme, and may feel that the question is therefore solved. If we believe this, we shall criticise atheistic groups such as Buddhists for not having the answer to life, the solution to Creation. This is true, because Buddhism does not concern itself with speculation, or base itself on belief. Instead it tries to encourage people to find things out from personal experience, from living. We all have life, and we have to understand what it means. We may trace our lives back to when we were born, but is there any benefit in trying to understand the origins of our physical life? Supposing we could do so, would we get liberation from this? Would this provide the solution to a bad life, full of ignorance and suffering?

Instead of concerning ourselves with the origin of life, we have to understand life here and now. You may say that the present is related to the past, because what we are now is the result of what we have been. This is so, if we carry the past with us; and when we carry it with us it is working in the present. So the past can be looked at *now*. We have to see its workings for ourselves, using the investigative mind, and not relying upon what others say. This applies to everything we come across in life.

If we observe life we shall see that both external and internal conditions play an active role in life. Life continues in the universe according to certain laws. It is therefore never completely free from the conditions of the world; it has to conform in order to exist. One of the most famous laws is that of Cause and Effect. However, this is not a kind of determinism, because it is not rigidly followed in the sense that nothing can be otherwise. Determinism would mean unchangeability, whereas in life there is continual change. In reality there is choice, although this is conditioned by what we know, or what we desire. This is related to the Law of Kamma.

The Law of Kamma plays a very important role in

Buddhist life, but I feel that when we are considering the New Approach to Buddhism we should change the emphasis of some of the Buddhist doctrines, including this Law of Kamma. This law has been useful in creating values of life in the moral sense. But it also means the law of action and reaction in life, and these can in fact come to an end.

We have to understand that anything we take into ourselves which can strengthen the ego, makes liberation more difficult and must be put aside. In Buddhism there is one meaning of Kamma which we tend to overlook: that is the action which brings about the end of action. Such action is not a kind of accumulation—it works in the opposite direction. Normally we try to accumulate knowledge, or security, because of the tendency to have, to show ourselves and others that we have. But the action that leads towards the end of action is the true type of action, and may sometimes appear as inaction. Action does not have to mean doing something, producing something. Doing nothing, *being* nothing, has immense power because through it arises the understanding of the meaning of life. Confusion and delusion disappear, but may arise again when we return to the thinking mind because of the rush of ideas and conflicting elements within us. If we can go beyond the thinking mind, illusion will dissolve. People may ask whether Buddhism believes that life or the world is an illusion. But Buddhism does not base itself on beliefs. It is not a matter of answering the question but of developing one's own insight, when it will be seen that the question is not put rightly.

The action that brings about the end of action is the real action in life. How can society progress if such action is going to bring it to an end? If you go into this deeply, you will be able to understand it—it will come to you. Such action does not aim at accumulation, but is concerned with itself. What we do is completely done; what we live is completely lived; what we experience is completely experienced. There is no grasping, no holding on, no carrying on. Everything is done for its own sake, and we are free from what we have done. We do not identify ourselves with our work, status, or position in life. When there is no identification, we are free to do, with understanding, wisdom, the whole being. We do not do something by impulse but with clarity of understanding, and in this way we do nothing wrong in life—there is not even the concept of wrong, or right, in our behaviour, or laws of morality with which to conform. Otherwise we are dependent upon rules in order to live, to be good, to be happy. Such dependence cannot bring us to freedom.

What then is our guide? There must be something to help us over what is right and what is wrong, what should or should not be done. And that something should not be complicated to find. Perhaps you can guess what it is: it is *insight*. Clear insight into things, into reality, can be found within us—and it is the only true guiding principle, illuminating all situations without preconceived ideas, or even perceptions, because perception is related to recognition. Notion, concept, impression, image—none are required. Then the doors of perception are closed at a certain level, and the doors of insight open, giving light, clarity, understanding, freedom and love. Insight is the greatest treasure in life—in fact, real life is that. Insight is 'contained' in life, but I do not wish this to sound as if life is an object, a large object, which contains things! It is not something in which something else can be contained, yet it has everything—within and outside it. In fact there is no inward or outward in life; we just think about it in that way.

The action that brings an end to action is the action of true living—not the action of ego, which always brings about something else: progress, results, conflict, and so on. Ego is complicated and limited—it cannot work beyond itself. When we understand it, we have compassion for it, so we leave it alone! Do not try to destroy it, even if you want to do this because it seems to create so many problems. However, it is important to watch all its activities, to observe how it works, because in order to be free from ego one has to understand it.

This is part of the New Approach. Previously there has been a tendency to have a negative attitude towards ego—a wish to attack it, to kill it. This is because of an inability to really see what it is, to grasp it. In fact, it cannot be killed. Perhaps instead we should dissolve the idea of the ego, not by destroying it but by giving it up. How do we give it up? First we have to understand how the idea is formed. Once an image has been formed about yourself, you are limited, like narrowing yourself to a small and muddy pond— the water has become dirty because it has no outlet— and you, living in it, may think 'Oh, this is a marvellous place!' Like a frog, who does not realise how different his pond is from the sea, because he has never seen the sea. Life has to flow into the depths and vastness of true living, free from the image of self. The image is the plan of the ego—we have a personality programme to be something, and this limits us. In order to reach the sea from our small pond, we have to flow like a river.

In that flow, we shall encounter suffering sometimes. But why should we avoid suffering if it has to come? If we let it come and see how it operates, we can use it. Life without suffering while we are still on the path would have no meaning, and insight would never become deep. However, sorrow must come to an end, and in the process of life happiness will arise as well as suffering. If we do not experience them both consciously, they will be experienced unconsciously, unknowingly. This is because life has to flow, and if it does not flow positively it will build up a negative power, creating obstruction and conflict which is experienced as suffering. After it has been expressed as suffering, there may be a period of relief or pleasure, but this repeated cycle is unconscious and therefore does not lead to liberation. However, if we understand the nature of obstructions and allow them to drop away through the exercise of awareness, watching suffering and joy arise and fall, these cycles will lead us gradually through more subtle barriers to more subtle depths of life, until we reach the sea. That is the Deathless Death, the ending of the rivers, the ending of becoming.

This does not mean that somewhere there exists an end for life to reach, so that we look towards this end instead of living life from moment to moment, here and now. Many people want to be happy after death, or live in 'Heaven', on a higher plane of existence because they have done good in this life and they believe in the Law of Kamma. But this is a prolongation of the ego, and the self does not come to an end. That is why I say we need to change the emphasis. Teachings about rebirth have to be put aside for a while. Instead of thinking about what happens to life after death we should concern ourselves with what happens to life here and now. See this clearly first, and then it will be realised what life after death really means. Rebirth is in this life.

We can look at it in two ways. The first is that rebirth is a process of dying and being reborn in life, from moment to moment, and through this process there is becoming and continuity. There are certain conditions sustaining this process, so we are not free from the law of cause and effect. But if the mind understands these conditions it lets them come and go—like the rain which came yesterday and went today. We can become more and more free from the conditions of life, coming and going, but we work our way, living life fully from moment to moment. Then we understand that the true end of life is in the living, not somewhere 'out there', not an idea existing in the mind or in scriptures. So we live life understanding its activity and movement.

The second meaning of rebirth is to die to all complicated, destructive, negative things, and even to positive things—to die to everything, and to be reborn into a new dimension of life. Without such a death, we can never be reborn into such a dimension, because we shall have the old things with us all the time: getting up in the morning, seeing the same thing, having breakfast, going to the office, coming back home, thinking the same thoughts, reacting to things in the same way in a dull, routine life. In this way we find nothing interesting in life because we are not reborn into new dimensions, new perceptions. If we can die to the past and live fully in the present we shall see everything differently, being sensitive to our surroundings and to ourselves, with a feeling of going more deeply into life.

At any moment we may have a deeper experience of life, during any of our daily activities, but we must have the means for this. The means are simple, yet not easy; this is because of our habit of overlooking their simplicity. Also, we often set a low value upon simplicity, believing that important matters must be more complex.

Awareness is simplicity itself. Through awareness we can understand the true meaning of life and death, because they are two poles of living, two aspects of the same process. And when we fully understand them we shall fear neither life nor death, remaining free within the purity of living.

II

INTEGRATION OF THE INTELLECTUAL AND THE SPIRITUAL LIFE

YOU HAVE OFTEN listened to a man in robes, and today it may be different listening to a man in civilian clothes, so I should like to explain my position a little as many people may not have heard what I was going to do.

Robes are a symbol, a form, and when we put them on we are in a certain role where we try to conform to an ideal or to rules without looking into all aspects of life. It therefore fragments life, creating a division between the holy and the ordinary, and tends to prevent the individual from experiencing the wholeness of life. People think that the holy man should be dressed in a certain way, and they link holiness with form. This is contrary to reality, because in reality the holy is very ordinary, very simple. When we overlook simplicity we shall not find the holy, but instead just find the idea of holiness and worship this, in a religious way.

Nowadays in particular we see many people adopting a special way of dressing, often imitating the oriental styles, and this conditions the minds of people to think that something holy is very different from life in general. Holiness is then sought externally, in a form, instead of within us. In order to be integrated we should not wear a special uniform but something ordinary, yet live the true life—then there will be holiness in everything. Holy means wholeness, integration, and this does not exist in ideals, in forms. It is found in the everyday practice of life, from moment to moment, without giving room for past or future.

You may think that without attention to the future there will be no progress in life. But the future is only a concept, a thought about time. When one can live the present fully, it extends itself to the future because the present is not something limited, placed between past and future. It is the wholeness of time; the moment in which there is no separation, no distinction, no representation, and no symbolism. So if we can live fully, from moment to moment, we can understand the treasures of life without reliance upon form. Life is wonderful, and interesting, containing an endless variety of negative and positive things which we have to go through, as human beings. In order to understand the truth we also have to go through ourselves, because the truth is both within and outside us. It may be in front of us, beside us, within us—anywhere, but nowhere in particular. There is no fixed place for reality.

This is why integration is so important, especially the integration of intellectual and spiritual life.

Life appears to be divided into many compartments, with many roles, such as family life, office life, factory life, political life, economic life, personal life, and so on. These often conflict with one another because the same person may be playing different roles, living different lives, according to different ideas. Stress and contradiction arise because people identify with their roles and ideas and lose the meaning of living, of real being. Is there real being of myself at all? We always have many such questions, because we do not understand the wholeness of life. Instead we are immersed in disharmony and disintegration.

Before discussing the integration of intellectual and spiritual life we should examine the function of the intellect, and what is meant by spiritual life.

As you know, the intellect can perform like a computer, working out what has been put into it. Without information, intellect cannot work anything out, but you could use your intellect for a hundred years without reaching Truth. A Zen master once gave an analogy of scratching a foot with the shoe still on—instead of scratching the foot one will always scratch the shoe. This applies when we use intellect to understand reality. Not only do we not reach the truth, but we can distort it, because the intellect creates an image of truth, just as it creates an image of God. It cannot understand what truth is. It deals only with views, thoughts and ideas, and perceptions.

Concerning perception, you perceive according to how you feel. Feeling is the immediate condition of perception. Suppose you have a negative feeling about something, your perception will be coloured by this attitude. This particularly applies in human relations, in which the mood of the perceiver greatly influences the way another person is perceived. That is why the Buddha taught that we should be aware of our feelings.

Whenever there is contact, physically or through the mind, there is feeling and sensation immediately, after which perception arises, giving ideas and building up attitudes towards what is perceived. A whole series of mental formations come to be because of feelings and perceptions. If we can stop ourselves at the point of feeling, of experiencing, we shall not be led into distortion. Feeling comes and goes, like a bubble. If you watch the waves in the sea you will see bubbles appearing and disappearing. Feelings and sensations are like that.

In order to stop ourselves at the feeling or the sensation, we have to be very aware at the moment it arises. We must not jump over into thinking, otherwise we take everything in without knowing it and they enter the unconscious mind, accumulating there. This is because we are not sufficiently attentive to what is happening. Later we may become aware of this accumulation in the psyche without being aware of how it got there. One of the purposes of meditation is to improve the power of attention to what is happening, to be aware of our mechanisms and mannerisms. Only then is there any possibility of alternative behaviour.

Knowledge arises through perception, and knowledge can poison the mind if it is not digested. We have a stream of impressions coming through our senses, and if these flow into the mind without awareness it is dangerous. If awareness stands at the door of the senses, we can protect ourselves and other people.

Thought is another function of intellect. What is thinking? What happens when we think? Thinking may be the reaction to memory, which is flowing in the mind continually. The attention reacts to certain parts of this flow, according to interest at the time. Memories, whether recent or in the more distant past, provide a challenge to the mind, activating it into thinking. The thoughts which arise may range from fleeting associative thought to more intense, sustained thinking, depending upon the circumstances. They can also arise from the events of life, concerning people, objects, or problems, which throw up a more forceful challenge to the mind.

The usual mental reaction is based on ideas and attitudes. You can notice this when sitting down to meditate; if a noise occurs you may react with irritation because you had the idea of quietness, the idea of being free from noise, the attitudes that things should be so, or not so. But if you have no preconceived ideas you will not mind what happens; you just note it and leave it there, remaining free to continue being aware. In this way, everything that occurs is experienced as part of you, not separate, not disruptive. If I wish to pay it attention I do so; if not, I do not. I am free to choose which I shall do. This freedom arises through non-reaction, which can only come about in the absence of preconceived ideas.

Such freedom of mind is different from thought, and is also beyond the interference of views, which is another aspect of intellect. Views are formed according to our conditioning, our education, our background, and all our past experience. We have certain views on certain things, because of inner conditions. Views are often speculative, very different from the pure seeing of something. This meaning of view refers to the seeing of reality as it is: pure vision, unconditioned by thought.

So intellect works with perceptions, thoughts and views. We do not reject all this entirely, and should not wish to destroy it, because we must have perceptions, thoughts and views, and deal with the facts in life. Without factual knowledge and conceptualisation, our minds would not be able to work, and without factual memory we could not function in daily life. However, we should be able to detach from the intellect, and let it lie still so that it can receive signals without distortion. This is the ground of spiritual life.

Spiritual life refers to purity of heart, holiness, or wholeness of being, without which we do not really live—we merely exist day by day without touching the depths of life, remaining only on a superficial level. Actually, the superficial and the deep can run along together, like relative truth and ultimate truth. In life we have to accept both forms: conventional, which is relative, and the ultimate. On the relative plane we have to accept a man as a man, a woman as a woman, things as they appear. Yet at the same time we can experience them differently: a man as not a man. This sounds contradictory, confusing—but it is only the 'I' which becomes confused. When seeing both forms of truth at the same time, the 'I' is not there, it has been abandoned, leaving only the understanding of what is. There is no seer, no perceiver, no knower. At that point there is no conflict.

You may ask how one can reach this point, believing it to be very deep or very high. No, as I said before, holiness is very ordinary and simple—it is in life. It is in seeing and understanding, not in perception and thinking, unless our thought is free and without bias. This is thinking from the heart, not from the head. This kind of heart is the crux of being, but we do not ask where it is because such questions are the work of intellect. Put intellect aside, and then awareness will flow between inner and outer, depth and superficiality, spirituality and intellectuality, bringing insight to the surface.

When the intellect is quiet and still, it can receive the meaning of life. It does not exercise itself in thinking, speculation, comparison, measurement, or anything apart from merely receiving. After periods of such receptivity it can think in a different way—in fact, it becomes highly intelligent, because through pausing it can see much more deeply. Its logic becomes more subtle and profound, and forms a sound basis for further discovery. In this way insight and intellect can work together.

Spirituality does not necessarily exist in the church, temple, monks or priests—it exists everywhere, in everyone, both within and outside us.

When we look within ourselves we understand what we have, how we become, what we are. We can see our conditioning, our thinking, our behaviour—and the deeper internal conditions which influence all our actions. This is first-hand knowledge, 'inside' knowledge, without being taught. It is our own seeing and intelligence which gives us the understanding. Intelligence means the capacity to think objectively, yet it comes from the heart, unlike intellect which can become very hard sometimes because it is divorced from feeling. The heart is always gentle, even, sensitive and true. The heart is spiritual, the head is intellectual. But they have to work together. To work only with the heart can produce a foolish good man, the 'stupid saint'. The head must work with the heart to result in wisdom. When we understand how the head works we can have integration between head and heart.

We can be perfect human beings, using everything we have. We are free to use all that is there, or not. Through integration of the head and the heart, the intellectual and the spiritual, there is no conflict between them. Apparent contradictions arise because things are seen on different levels. I may say that this glass in front of me is a glass in the conventional sense, but not a glass when seen from a different aspect. You may be able to accept these conflicting statements because you understand different levels, and this frees the mind from the tendency to reject, or dogmatically believe. It is no use just grasping words without seeing meaning—this leads to confusion. When we are not attached to words, yet through them can see the meaning, the inner content. One of the Buddha's greatest disciples, Sariputta, when he was a young man searching for truth, came across a monk called Assaji walking in a town collecting alms. Sariputta felt that this man had the answer to what he was looking for, but not wanting to disturb him he walked at some distance behind him. When the monk left the town he approached him to ask about his teaching. The monk perceived great intelligence in the young man, and told him he was very new to the teaching and could not tell him much. Sariputta told him he did not mind about the words—he just wanted their meaning. The monk then said a few words, and the young man understood their meaning. He later met the Buddha and became a great disciple, of the greatest wisdom, on the right hand of the Buddha.

Words can become an obstacle to the understanding of their meaning, because we tend to conceptualise, to have ideas and notions, making the head so busy that it prevents the heart from working. That is why the Buddha warned against getting stuck in words, otherwise one becomes like an elephant in the mud, unable to move. Words are part of the play of the intellect. We justify arguments by saying that the meanings of words have to be clarified before we can understand. The whole school of philosophy emphasising linguistic analysis has remained powerful for many years in England because of this idea, and has succeeded in blocking the mind, limiting it to the study of concepts and words.

It is true that one needs to explore the meaning of what is said, and avoid 'woolly' expressions, but such investigation must be combined with experience, not conjecture. Several books have been written concerning the concept of self by philosophers who do not take the trouble to really look inwards at themselves. Such direct experience is rejected by them as being 'subjective'—but endless theorising and intellectual discussion cannot lead to objective truth.

True enquiry can never be a matter for the intellect only. Supposing a negative feeling arises in you, and you wish to discover what it is and how it arose, it is not a question of analysing the words with which you describe it, it is a matter of looking into the state itself, seeing it clearly. Only then will the facts come to light.

Man has to work to carry on life and society, and in fact he already possesses all that is needed for fulfilment of life. If he can reach integration, this will release creative energy for his work. But usually this energy is dispersed through the fragmentation of our personality, giving rise to exhaustion, a feeling of lifelessness, depression. We continually make distinctions, comparisons, and measurements. In particular, we measure ourselves according to our aspirations and our knowledge. The Buddha has said we measure ourselves from a state of sleep, from dullness, so that we measure things from ignorance. Thus we build up a false image of ourselves. People say that the real self is lost. Why is it lost? Because we identify ourselves with the role we play, our status, so that we do not know what we are. We think we *are* businessmen, scientists, artists.

You may think this role-playing is only a game—we can play and then stop playing. But this identification can become deeply rooted, preventing us from coming to our real selves, wholeness, integration.

Life is a formless form—it cannot be put into words. Life is not confined to a house, a street, but everywhere, fully accessible to the integrated man. The integrated man is aware—awareness is the only way leading to harmony within man. A man cannot ask someone to make him integrated. He has to do this for himself, through sensitivity, attentiveness, alertness. When we are drowsy and dull, we have to be aware of this and watch it, however heavy it is, just acknowledging it. Then things will come up, telling us what we need to know. It is a very simple process, and simplicity is profound.

We find it difficult to think simply, and dwell instead on what is complicated, but this leads towards disintegration. The path to integration of the spiritual and the intellectual is a simple one, even though it may be difficult.

QUESTIONER: Can we think of purifying the mind in terms of a self-cleaning machine?

DHIRAVAMSA: The mind is cleansed through the process

of awareness. When it becomes aware of itself it penetrates into its own conditions, and by doing that it is purifying itself. Therefore it is true that it cleans itself, but not mechanically, like a machine. It is not automatic. It cleanses itself of impurities, disturbances and defilements. But there must be a means, and as the Buddha said, awareness is the only way, leading to realisation, enlightenment, seeing things as they really are. There is no other way, and this way covers the whole field of life.

We can be aware of anything, but we must let it grow, day by day, when we shall become clear in our thinking, our perceiving. Normally we do not perceive clearly because the mind is so occupied and so dull that we cannot see things, their beauty. We cannot see what beauty is. We may see it only in forms, in shapes, but not the pure beauty which is both with and without form.

III

FREEDOM AND LOVE

I WONDER whether we are free to talk and to listen to the topic we are going to discuss this evening: Freedom and Love. If we are not free, we may not be able to do so. It is essential to be free from the beginning to listen and to talk, and also to be silent, so that we can understand the subject.

Firstly we should look at what freedom is, but we cannot give it a definition. It limits something to give it a definition, because one tends to stay with the words without penetrating beyond them to the meaning. Or people cling to ideas or feelings aroused by words, and instead of seeing the whole field of what is spoken about, they confine themselves to only a part. This is how we become closed. We hold on to certain ideas and meanings, not being prepared to explore the matter in greater depth.

Therefore we start by leaving the subject undefined, by not saying 'freedom is this, freedom is not that'. It is human conscience which can understand what freedom is—human commonsense can explore this. That conscience or commonsense must be pure and alone within itself, unconditioned by background and thought which usually govern what we *call* conscience. One may wonder whether such a different kind of conscience is possible, because we are conditioned from the beginning and are not really free. But perhaps awareness of this conditioning and lack of freedom will open the way towards freedom. If we understand how we are conditioned, how we become closed to other ideas or to everything we come across in life, then from there it may be possible to have a glimpse of freedom.

If we are not free, we have to look and see the cause for this. We see ourselves as entities, wanting to be free, and also wanting to *be* something in order to have freedom, and it is this which gives rise to difficulty in being free. There are many things involved in this process of having freedom. Suppose we are listening to someone talking and we can see how we react to what is being said, or to the speaker. If we watch these reactions or responses to what is going on now, we may be able to see whether we are free to listen or whether we are listening with certain ideas, motives, or attitudes. We may be listening with expectancy, or with a critical mind, trying to prove whether the speaker is right or what is being said is true. In that case, we are not free. If we are free we do not try to analyse what is being said, but just listen, and let the listening take care of itself. Then the mind is free and flowing with this freedom of listening, so there is no obstacle standing in the way.

It is essential to understand this kind of freedom. The main obstruction is the self, because the self has certain attitudes, ideas and thoughts. The self has patterns of thinking, feeling and perceiving. But although the self is limited, it is dynamic and can therefore break away from its own limitations. This is made difficult, however, when the self has become static and enclosed by its accumulation of experience, when it becomes the greatest obstacle to freedom.

You might then say 'I must have freedom from the self', but if another self desires freedom we may then have two selves, both wanting something. If it is the desire of the self to be free, there will be no freedom, because the first freedom is freedom from desire. If we aim to be free through desire, we shall carry the wrong thing with us on our path, and the whole problem of desire will not be faced. In the end we have to work out how to be free from desire, even the desire to be free. This is not complicated, although words make it sound so. When we come to use words we have to be very careful because they can cause the intellect to think in a particular way which creates confusion.

The best way is to think from our experience, and have periods in which we are free from the mind, even if not for very long. During these times one can watch tensions and disturbance in an objective way, or can see states of well-being, ease, vitality, or of *being* without any image of self or identity. In these states there is tranquillity, serenity, clarity, alertness, and full understanding of what is really going on, and what is not. At the same time, there is a feeling of liberation and detachment, not in the sense of laziness and non-involvement but in the sense of being free from care. This detachment comes together with clear understanding. It is like a deep, tranquil lake, in which the water is very still and clear, without wind on the surface, and the whole atmosphere is silent. The mind can reach such a moment of tranquillity, in which you also move in the silence without physical movement, and such a mind can understand the depths of its own being.

This is a state of freedom, but like all states it must pass, and we become aware of the wish to be free from something. We may say there are two steps: the first is to be free from something, and the second is to be free to be, to act, to move, to do anything without obstruction. How can we take these steps? We may feel it is of the greatest importance to do so, understanding that it is freedom which gives meaning to life. How can we get it?

First of all we have to see why we do not have freedom. Instead of striving to gain freedom we must become aware of what is the matter. We have to put this question to ourselves, and look. By looking fully into the causes and conditions, freedom will come. It is often because our attention is centred upon what we want that we fail to see what is really going on within us. Not only do we not see, but we repress what is there because our desires do not include it. We think we know what we want, and what we do not want, and the twin motives of acquisition and avoidance cause us to bypass what is. At the same time, at some level we have a degree of awareness of the situation, so that the mind remains unsatisfied, restless and depressed. This is part of a vicious circle, because the wish to avoid unhappiness intensifies the search for happiness, in the wrong direction. The drive to acquire is inseparably linked with the drive to avoid.

In turning towards pleasure in an attempt to relieve the mind of suffering generated by the suppression of what is, we only reinforce that suppression because we are avoiding the core of the problem. This cannot lead to an understanding of the mind; instead it strengthens a pattern of behaviour, of escape, of unconsciousness, which must lead to further suffering.

How can this continuing cycle of avoidance and suffering be broken? By looking, at every opportunity, and by conscious action. We may sometimes see clearly that a certain direction, although the hardest, is the best and should be followed. Then we can be ruthless to the self-indulgent tendencies within us—but not obsessive, as this is just another form of indulgence. Freedom does not mean I can do what I like, nor does it mean a compulsion to do what I do not like. Both are slavery to a superimposed wish, whereas freedom starts from within and not from outside.

Social freedom is secondary to inner freedom. When we are inwardly free we shall discover freedom in the world, living among the demands and limitations of this world, yet without harm or loss. We do not look for freedom from outside: we have it within us, and then it is everywhere, with everything we do, with every person we meet, without being disturbed by anything.

If within ourselves there is disturbance and anxiety, we see the world as disturbed and disturbing—it is coloured by our state of mind; and also of course the events in society and the world are obviously affected by the state of individual minds. If inner disturbance is repressed, it becomes more deeply rooted in the mind and more difficult to deal with. We have to look and see what these disturbing things are, and how we are caught up in them and further conditioned by them.

We have the means for freedom, which are simple although not easy to practise constantly. I am speaking of awareness. As the Buddha said: 'This is the only way leading to realisation, to enlightenment, to overcoming all forms of suffering.' There is no other way. When we talk of 'the way of awareness' we do not mean that awareness is one thing and the way is another, or that there is a technique for applying awareness to life. Awareness *itself* is the doing, the practice, the action—there is no technique for being aware.

Awareness cannot flow without simplicity in life. What is simplicity? To be simple is not to look for help or for techniques, but at what is going on now. You can go to it directly instead of asking for guidance, and then you will see that freedom is the first and last factor in the practice of awareness. If one depends upon techniques to produce awareness one cannot practise awareness itself, diving inwards to see what is there or opening outwards to look at everything one comes across. Very often we rely upon conviction about what we are going to do before we can do it, but this is a result of fear of the unknown, of the unbelieved. Fear is the greatest obstacle to freedom. We cannot dissolve fear immediately, so we must suspend it while we explore our situation.

Fear is in fact the greatest problem in everybody's life, although sometimes it is so subtle that it becomes almost invisible. Throughout life there is fear: fear of loss, of being deprived, of not having support, of not obtaining what is needed or wanted, of meeting people who may do harm, either real or imaginary. In general, there is fear of living, because life can give and take at any moment, irrespective of the defences we build around ourselves. Closely linked with the fear of living is the disguised fear of enlightenment, because we realise on a deeper level that this will mean the dissolution of the self which we spend our lives defending and creating. This is why we so often slow down at the moment when we should be making progress in our practice of awareness, or we fail to grasp opportunities which arise in our lives but do not remain and may not reappear for many years.

When we observe the many forms of fear arising in us, can we see what conditions give rise to them? Fear is not possible unless the mind is holding onto something which gives it security, but which can be threatened because its nature is not permanent or free.

It may be an idea, or a hope concerning something it seeks, or a belief in its own meaning or worth. From this state of possession, it wants to possess more and more. To go into reverse and possess less, wish for less, requires a movement in the opposite direction from the automatic one. This may seem difficult at first, because it is different from the usual tendency towards attachment. We are attached to what we have—whether to friends, to objects, to children, to husband or wife, to the body, and above all to the mind itself—and any move to disengage ourselves from these things will cause fear.

Another factor that makes detachment difficult is that the attachment to things brings with it a type of pleasure, and becomes what we believe to be essential for our happiness. Also attachment goes very deep; it is a form of conditioning which penetrates to a profound level in many subtle disguises. It cannot just be discarded or rejected, however. When I say that attachment is the cause of fear, this does not mean that attachment is 'wrong' in every way—it cannot be uprooted suddenly, or resisted. This creates a negative attitude towards attachment, and we become attached to this attitude. If possible we should not give a concept to attachment, or let any concept of it impress us, and the same applies to desire.

When fear arises because of attachment, what should we do? Do nothing, nothing at all, except see it clearly. When we see it with the eye of wisdom, directly, without any doubt, then that seeing itself will lead to freedom. That is why I say do not do anything—otherwise you invite trouble! Seeing is action, understanding is action. Yet we still feel we must act, we *must* act. This is our trouble. We cannot be passive in the right way, when action takes place of its own accord. Our own activeness becomes the obstacle to liberation. This does not mean that we should sit back passively doing nothing in every sphere of life.

Passivity is relevant to our release from attachment, but when dealing with material things we cannot be entirely passive. We need to be active, but not over-active. So there must be a balance between activeness and passiveness in life, knowing when to be active and when to be passive. How can we know? There is no formula to give, but awareness of the situation will always show us the right way, and through insight we can approach life in a balanced state of mind. With a clear and alert mind, the body is sensitive and receptive, without dullness or heaviness, and this in turn lightens the mind, relieving it of thought, so that it is free to think, or not to think. Sometimes you may think that you are free to think, but not free not to think. We have to understand why this is.

If we try to get rid of fear through effort, we shall distract our energy into an activity which is based on avoidance, or rejection. This only strengthens fear. You may say we can therefore do nothing about this situation, but we can do something. Earlier I said we should do nothing, and now I seem to contradict myself by saying that we can do something. But what we can do has the nature of non-action: that is, we can be aware of fear—how it arises, how it operates, and how it ends. This is passive activity: watching, looking, not only on the surface but into deeper levels of fear, so that you can see the underlying conditions. If you practise awareness everything will be revealed—and this is the true meaning of revelation. We uncover the covered; and in most people the greatest part of their mind is usually covered, unconscious, so that they cannot understand it. Enlightenment simply means that we uncover the covered, and put away the lids! Then everything remains clear.

Now we shall talk about love. What is love? Again, we shall not give ourselves any definition. Love is inseparable from freedom—without freedom there is no love. We cannot love anyone or anything if we are not free. The love we are speaking of is not an emotional reaction; we shall not divide it into devotional love, possessive love, sexual love, or whatever, but we shall keep it as simply love. But in that love there is everything—nothing is lacking. Where love is in a particular category, there is no fullness, no completion—there is something lacking. It is the same with life, when it is divided into different compartments, out of harmony with each other, often seeming hollow. When integrated, however, it all flows together, full of life.

Love is everywhere. Christianity teaches that God is everywhere, and God is love. If we understand this fully, we can see love everywhere, in everything.

In distinguishing freedom from love, we may see that freedom is the non-active aspect of reality, whereas love is active. With love we move freely because we are supported by freedom underlying the movement. If thought interferes, we become blocked or even paralysed. Love is distorted by ideas or beliefs, and the freedom of action is impeded. This is recognised even in ordinary language when we say that when we think too much we cannot act. Doubts arise as to whether one is wrong or right, or what will be the results of an action. On the question of war, for instance, and how to put an end to it, someone may have different attitudes, principles, or a certain ideology which leads to indecision.

When we love, we can move. Love is the movement of the heart, and in the heart. It is the movement itself—it is not that the heart moves in order to have love, or that love is something moving in the heart. But there is a kind of movement, and when we have love we can feel it in the heart, in the middle of ourselves—not in the physical heart. Love is not attachment, because the heart is free, released.

Love can be both personal and impersonal. You may say that love can be limited and unlimited. This depends upon how we look at love. Love itself is neither limited nor unlimited, but it seems to be when looked at from different points of view. The love of a mother and child, or husband and wife, appear limited because it is personal. But we can love a particular object or person without excluding ourselves, and also the love will spread itself through an object to reach a broader field. This is why love must flow unhindered. It can become impersonal and comprehensive as long as we do not say 'this is my love'. The idea of me and mine should not be there.

What happens when we love? There is caring, responsibility, or the ability to respond to the needs of another individual, of society, of humanity. If you respond positively, there is love; if you respond negatively, love cannot flow—this is obvious. What else happens when there is love? There is understanding, which removes conflict and confusion, not by force which suppresses movement. Understanding is the basis for true relationships, and we cannot live without some relationship. The Buddha said, 'Good companionship is the whole of the holy life'. So the holy life does not exist without good relationship, and this is why I often call the holy life the ordinary life. It is ordinary because of its simplicity. There is no idea of inferiority or superiority. Put these concepts aside; live a simple life, and see the holiness in it. Then we shall not be conditioned by what we 'know', whether it is wrong or right. We have to be free from what we know. Otherwise we are conforming to ideas, to what is said or read.

With freedom and love, human beings will have a true relationship, both personal and impersonal. Good companionship does not mean the opposite to something bad or evil. It is good because there is goodness within itself. Good companionship is something united in the freedom of relationship. We cannot escape relating to people and things, but we are influenced by the attitudes, reactions and behaviour of others and cannot be 'alone' within the relationship. This does not mean that we are cut off or remote. No, we are there, completely there, but are alone in the sense of non-attachment to the things we are with. We have insight into a relationship, without condemning or blaming or exalting ourselves or others. In this case there is no image of the relationship—we come to it in the here-and-now, in being. We see beyond the mask, or personality, to the real being of a person. Human beings are complicated in their expressions and manifestations, but on a deeper level there is no complexity, no conflict.

You may ask why it is that people present such a complicated picture when in reality their true nature is simple. It is because of the impressions and intrusions

33

upon the mind made by the senses and by the activity of the mind itself, which accumulates experience. The unconscious mind causes conflict and complication, but it is comparatively near the surface of man, not in the depths. It belongs to the sphere of becoming, not of being. All becoming belongs to the surface, although there may be different levels of this surface. It depends upon our analysis. In order to get to the depths, we have to go through these levels and become aware of them. In order to be free, we have to go through all that we are not free from. So do not reach for freedom without dealing with what is there within you. Otherwise your work will remain in the field of expectancy, and this robs you of energy. If we live in a world of fantasy and hope, we shall let our energies flow in that direction and have none left for work with what is actual. We find ourselves back in the world of desire. Even when working with facts, we may do it in order to gain certain results—once again with an eye to the future instead of insight into the present.

If we deal with the present, the future takes care of itself. Expectation is irrelevant. The natural law means that where there is action there is reaction in accordance with it. If we understand this law we shall not waste energy in looking towards the future, discussing it. Instead we shall remain silent, and use our energy in the present. Silence, in an inward mental sense, is the greatest source of energy there is.

Silence does not only occur in an obvious way, but also in fleeting moments between actions and even between each thought. In the balance between silence and energy, love can flow. If we are preoccupied by things in life, we cannot experience its flow. The movement of the sea cannot be seen with the naked eye because its motion is deep. The movement of love in our hearts is not perceived by the superficial conditioned mind.

Love is without expectation. Relationships are not based on getting something in return. That is not relationship, but the destruction of relationship.

IV

ANATTĀ—NO-SELF

ANATTĀ IS the Pali term for No-Self. This may seem a very dry subject to discuss, and in fact often frightens people, because normally they have a strong feeling of self. Even at the time of the Buddha, people were afraid of his teaching of *anattā*. Usually people have to feel they are somebody, otherwise they find it difficult to live. Actually, any statement that there is no self goes to one extreme, and the statement that there is a self goes to the other extreme. The first is an annihilist idea, and the second is eternalist in the sense that the self is regarded as a permanent entity. Because Buddhism is the Middle Way, it teaches that the mind should not become attached to belief in either of these two extremes. This is the way of balance.

But what can we say, if neither view can be held? If I say either, I shall be an extremist, not a Buddhist, so what is the truth? The fact is that there is conditionality in things as they are. Everything comes to be because of certain conditions, and then ceases to be because of other conditions. Nothing can be completely grasped and no-one can grasp it. Things are as they are.

I do not want to go into the theory of *anattā*. Most of us have read something on the subject in books written by learned Buddhists. But what we talk about now should be something which relates to our actual experience, and based on putting the teaching into practice in life. I feel it is a waste of time to merely learn the doctrine of *anattā*, or try to prove one or another view about the subject of self. This type of intellectual Buddhism, which is little more than a display of knowledge to show scholastic status, does not help us in life. We do not live according to what we know, so what is the point of gaining knowledge, accumulating information, continuing to speculate? We must not waste our time.

We have to understand why the Buddha taught

anattā. Perhaps one reason was because it was such a central factor in his teaching of the truth that nothing can be permanent, nothing can be absolute. It is a relative, conditioned world, in which everything is related and nothing can remain independent from other things. Human beings cannot exist alone, without dependence upon something else. If there is no relationship with the things of this world, there is no existence. This is obvious to all of us. It not only applies to actual existence, but to our affairs in life. Everything is interconnected, so that one activity or event will automatically affect another. The law of cause and effect governs the activity of everything.

When this is not understood, we seek permanence or the eternal, and if we are taught the doctrine of eternity we create an idea of this in our minds in terms of permanent time. Thus we limit the truth to concepts within time and space. But if we cease our thinking, time and space will disappear. When we think of 'now', we call it the *eternal* now, thus qualifying it into endless time. Similarly, the Buddhist goal of Nirvana is thought of as an eternal state. This is because of our limited understanding, so we have to look at things carefully to see whether they can be permanent or absolute.

Something called 'self' is sometimes thought to be an everlasting, unchanging entity, leaving the body and taking up another body, living many lives until it becomes completely purified. The self is also regarded as the feeler of feelings, the experiencer of experiences, the thinker of thoughts, the perceiver of the perceived. With our usual pattern of thought, we believe there are always two things: the seer and the seen, the thinker and the thought, in a subject-object relationship. Our language implies a subject and an object. But is language capable of expressing the truth, or is it only concerned with symbols of the truth?

When we say 'I am the thinker', what is the 'I'? The body? The mind? Or both? I cannot say what 'I am' means, but I have the feeling that the 'I' as thinker, perceiver, observer, listener, talker, cannot be grasped.

Who is the thinker? You may say 'the Buddha was a clear thinker', but perhaps the Buddha never thought at all, yet because his teaching was clear and helpful he has been described as a great man, a great thinker.

When you meditate, you may think there is a meditator, doing meditation. If this is so, the meditation is not properly done, because the self who is meditating is always in the way, creating problems, looking for results, hoping for experiences. The ego is always planning to be somebody, wanting to be recognised.

If we cannot really grasp the 'I' who is the thinker, the meditator, why do we still hold on to the idea of this entity? Maybe you are not aware of trying to hold on to it, but if you observe your behaviour you will find that it is largely concerned with the defence and support of the ego. You also *feel* your self. But if you look more attentively at the processes of feeling and thought, going more and more deeply into your observation, the image of self will disappear and there will be a great clarity of seeing, without a seer behind it. This may be a frightening experience for those experiencing it for the first time. 'Me' is lost, and until insight has strengthened there will be a tendency to try to regain it because of the feeling of insecurity. But in fact the 'me' must remain lost in order to rediscover what is real.

Who knows what the 'real self' is? If it can be defined, it is only an idea. If it can be recognised, it is something known by us already. The mind is expert at creating anything which maintains its own progress. It cannot exist without satisfying itself and the ego, by grasping and trying to maintain what supports it. But the real self is like no-self—free from grasping, and free from loss. At a psychological level, identity may be essential, but if we try to live on a wholly psychological plane we shall deceive ourselves and remain in illusion, thinking it is the truth, and living very superficially. It is the same with security. We may feel security with certain factors in life: good friends, a safe position, firm beliefs, a well-protected ego. But is such security valuable, or even desirable? It can screen us from the true nature of life, and it builds up dependence. We have no freedom, but are run by the ego and our psychological conditioning. These operate in us all the time, and unless they are dissolved we cannot come to freedom.

Freedom from the idea of self is the first step leading to liberation, and in order to dissolve this idea one has to be fully aware of the processes of 'me', 'my', and 'myself'. They are the product of time, the residue of *karma*, and create the problems of living. The conflicts of life arise from the 'me', which cannot live in the present fully but brings with it the past, because the 'me' itself has been created by the past. Anything 'me' feels or thinks must be conditioned by the past, and its eyes are blurred or blind because it always has to see from the angle of the past. Its entire range of perception is therefore distorted by conditioning, and it can never see things anew. This is why it can never see reality, or live in a fresh dimension.

You may take the view that because of past conditioning, what we have been determines what we are and there is no chance of freedom. Do you accept that? It may be said that there is no way out, and therefore it must be accepted. But this finalist way of thinking is not the Buddhist way, which regards change as the only thing in life which is certain. Everything fluctuates, and the power of awareness can change everything in the here and now. It is true that we are conditioned by the past, but this is because the past is here now, operating in us in the present, and is therefore not distant and inaccessible. It is operating at this moment in our feelings, thoughts, and behaviour. In order to have immediate access to the past, we have only to watch what is going on in the present. Patterns of reaction are conditioned by past experience, and intensive observation in the present will therefore clarify not only what your patterns are, but also reveal their sources. You will begin to understand your past existence as well as the present.

It is intensely interesting to learn about ourselves through the practice of watchfulness, without becoming fascinated or caught up in exciting ideas. The flow of watchfulness should continue to move in a flexible way, without getting clogged with thoughts and feelings. There must be a constant movement of observation, otherwise life cannot be understood. So do not try to reach the truth by reading books, such as the Tibetan Book of the Dead, which describes the realms through which dying people pass. On such information you may feel you know what happens to 'me', but it may be a teaching which is on the wrong basis.

Everything is within you, and all that must be done is to look at it, to be constantly aware of yourself in all situations, and then you will have knowledge which is not based on other people's experience and beliefs. When observing yourself, it is of the greatest importance to be honest, otherwise the understanding will be clouded. We try to avoid direct observation in many ways, and often by seeking knowledge from someone else. It is silly nonsense to search for true knowledge by going outside ourselves to other people. It is the typical behaviour of the conditioned mind which is afraid to look at itself, afraid to discover the truth. It is the activity of the 'me'. The 'me' will only disappear if we practise action without having the 'me' as its centre.

But how can this be done? First of all, leave the 'me' alone. You may see that the 'me' is the centre of all your thoughts, emotions and perceptions. O.K., it doesn't matter—let the 'me' do what it wants to do, but notice what it is doing. Deal with it gently and fairly, without aggression or violence. Do not try to destroy it, believing it to be 'bad', because this merely creates another problem, another area of rejection. We have enough problems of violence without adding another.

If we leave the 'me' alone we can then watch it in its activities—thoughts, perceptions, feelings. If we can see these processes as they are, and how they arise and disappear, we shall be able to understand the whole structure of the 'me' through its activities. In this way you will achieve understanding, and the centre of the 'me' you will find automatically disappears without any effort on your part to destroy it. This is because the 'me' has no real centre, and only exists at a superficial level. However, we cannot jump quickly to the depths but first have to go through all levels of the superficial, taking each process as it appears, using a simple approach of direct attention.

The method is simple, but this does not mean that the 'me' is easy to dissolve. We do not give up just because it is difficult. Instead, we look at the difficulties as they arise, and see why they are there. In this work, we do not look towards a goal, or a destination, but at the problem here, in front of us. When we become aware of difficulty, is it in fact a *feeling* of difficulty that we are experiencing? You already know that feeling is an activity of the 'me', and you will find that if you continue to look at feelings of difficulty they will disappear.

We should not overlook what is in front of us. Usually our attention is directed to something 'over there', or in the past or future, but this can be dangerous to us, and it is not easy to drop the habit. We have to watch what is happening *now*. If you say 'the me always interferes with my life', the 'my' indicates that it is the life of the ego. When you say 'my life' you are limiting yourself, and trying to act from the centre of the 'me' again. Life is life, not mine or yours. It is a moving reality, and has to flow without obstruction. It is like water moving along in a river, which sometimes gets stuck, or hindered by an obstacle in its way. It will be seen to churn, or 'struggle', because its nature is to flow. In fact it is not struggling, but its disturbance is a result of its need for movement. The force of life is the same, and when its flow is obstructed by the accumulation of mental contents suffering must arise.

It is suffering which can therefore awaken us to the fact that something is preventing the flow of life, and only by looking into the suffering, and the processes of 'me' which cause suffering, shall we be able to learn the lesson of life. If we are not aware of the suffering that is there, we shall never gain in wisdom, or have compassion for others. Awareness of suffering will show us the process of suffering, and we shall realise that there is no sufferer. Looking at this objectively will weaken the hold of the 'me' and lessen the image of a sufferer. Unless we can look at suffering objectively, without holding on to the idea of an entity who is suffering, it becomes very difficult to see what is happening. This is because 'the sufferer' is creating more obstacles.

One can feel very painful suffering, often appearing to be in the 'heart', which seems too intolerable to look at and which has to be repressed again and again. Many people start an avoidance pattern during childhood, when their parents taught them to ignore situations. Children are often discouraged from talking about what they think, or expressing what they feel, until they gradually lose their original awareness. If they were encouraged to look at everything that was happening, in a simple, direct way, they would have less tendency to develop unconscious fears and fantasies.

When turning away from the realities of life one is planting misery and illusion. The attempt to avoid the facts, to close the mind to actual feelings and thoughts, creates weakness and psychological problems. It is not the way to train oneself for life, or for death. In one of the Buddha's discourses on the development of the senses, we learn certain people at the time of the Buddha were trying to develop their senses by closing their eyes, mouth, ears, and nose, ignoring everything that was going on in the world. But the Buddha said that this only makes their senses dull; without exercising the senses, they atrophy, and cannot perceive what is actually there.

The Buddha's teaching was the opposite: be alert, and aware of what is going on, receiving all the impressions of life without trying to block them. When all perceptions occur receptively, with awareness, everything will be taken care of. When awareness is the doorkeeper, at the gate of the senses, perceiving will have clarity and tranquillity, without dullness or heaviness. There will then be no self-deception, delusion or hallucination.

Whatever we are working out, awareness should be present, and this especially applies to the investigation of the 'self'. The Buddha gave this important advice: 'Be a lamp unto yourself. Let the truth be your refuge, and nothing else.' He completely denied the existence of any self outside the body and mind, and told his followers to be a light unto themselves. You are your own light and protection—don't look for this externally, or it becomes an avoidance or defensive activity.

In Buddhism there is the injunction to take refuge in the Three Gems: the Buddha, the Dhamma and the Sangha—but they are really within us. If we put our trust in our image or idea of the Buddha, we shall be wasting our time. If we look for the Dhamma in scriptures or preachers, we shall never understand the Way. If we believe the Sangha is the external form, the monastic community, we shall not know what it truly means. Also, taking refuge does not mean the search for security through bolstering the ego—it means the discovery of what protection really is. We can gradually find that we are the Buddha, the Dhamma, and the Sangha. How? By following the Buddha's teaching of the cultivation of awareness, of all physical and mental processes. The whole universe is the object of our awareness. Do not give importance to the object—the essential thing is the awareness of whatever is there. It can be developed with any object, whether pleasant or unpleasant. If an object is painful to us, we have to continue to look at it; this is wisdom in action. All negative emotions, such as bitterness, resentment, envy, jealousy and fear, have to be observed as well as pleasurable or positive emotions. Also, we have to go through 'the Death' in life.

Thus the Buddha gave us the means for dissolving the idea of self. But this will not be achieved unless we attain to the First Stage on the path to enlightenment. At that moment we enter the Stream of Nirvana, when freedom from the idea of self is obtained. The only way to become such a 'Stream-winner' is through awareness and insight. How can we practise this awareness? By starting with our daily activities, from ourselves. If we think in terms of technique, we shall tend to stay with the *idea* of awareness, without entering the practice.

We should go direct to awareness, and not be afraid of doing something incorrectly. We are usually afraid of not doing the right thing, and cling to the idea that everything must be quite clear before we start. This type of perfectionism paralyses the natural flow of awareness, and prevents us from doing anything. All this is the activity of the 'me'.

Instead, try to attend to everything without judging your own abilities or criticising the weakness of your awareness. If you feel that you are failing, be aware of that feeling. Give your attention without hesitation to all that you experience, and do not waste time on regrets or disappointment if you do not succeed. Persistent application of your attention, even if it fluctuates, will gradually create greater sensitivity in you, and you will become aware more quickly of your distractions. As soon as you observe you have lost awareness, do not dwell on it, or complain, or become frustrated. Just return immediately to your work, because such feelings of disappointment are yet another distraction created by the self, carrying you away from what you are doing.

So whatever comes, just know it as it is. Do nothing else. In this way the 'me' is not able to persuade us to take its path, and we become more and more objective in our observation and thought. As we gradually gain freedom, the self has less and less place in our life, yet at the same time we see the self's processes with greater clarity. We see the two aspects of truth: conventional and ultimate. Conventionally speaking, there is 'me' and I accept this. However I do not cling to it, or work from its centre. I recognise it because I perceive it. But on the ultimate level, I know there is no 'me'. Because we live on different levels, there is no conflict. I conform to conventional conditions, for the sake of living and communicating; yet on another level I am free, being myself without having to be tied to the 'me'. Then I am in contact with my whole being, instead of the fragmented 'me'. The whole being is not *a* being, it is just *being*—complete being without an entity.

V

THE MEDITATIVE WAY OF LIFE

THE MEDITATIVE WAY OF LIFE may be different from
your ideas about it, so while listening to this talk it
would be a good idea not to have any idea! Then it
becomes easier to understand what we are talking
about. If we notice it in our life, we shall see that one
of the main difficulties in understanding something is
that we have preconceived ideas and cannot listen with
an open mind. There is already something in the mind
which prevents us from listening. We criticise, agree or
disagree, always reacting. Openness is the best way for
understanding and communicating. We are all working
together—the speaker and the listeners must communicate, silently. The speaker's voice may come out,
but he can be quiet inside and communicate with his
audience—otherwise he is speaking to himself, carrying
his own image to show off. This is not the real mission
of a speaker. He has to lose his own image, and really
become the talking. There is no talker behind the
talking, and then we are not talking according to ideas
but letting things flow and come out naturally. If they
do not come out we must not be disappointed, but
remain free. This is the task for all of us.

The meditative 'way' of life does not mean the
method, the school or the technique. I do not know
why we call it the way, but we have to use words in
order to communicate. The way means the living, or
the practice of life. So it means the living of life
according to meditation. We have to understand what
meditation is. This would be very difficult without
understanding what it is not. The negation of meditation is the meditation. The complete denial of all forms
of meditation is the meditation. So long as we practise
meditation according to a form, a technique, we are
not really meditating, but *trying* to. When the forms
disappear and we are left completely alone, then we
begin to meditate. You may say that we have a Medita-

tion Centre at which a certain technique is practised and taught to people, and in that case people who come to such a centre are not meditating. That is true. Not all of them can meditate, but they learn to meditate. A meditation centre is provided for people to learn how to meditate. However, learning in this case is not a kind of accumulating process. Instead, we learn in the sense of finding out why it is difficult to meditate, and what are the hindrances, all our psychological barriers, all the walls set against meditation. These obstacles have to be dissolved, otherwise meditation cannot come to be.

Meditation is not a magic or mystical way in which things seem mysterious or secret. That is the way people generally think of it. It is also not confined to certain people. It is actual awareness in life—the constant movement of awareness. This goes into life, all its activities. It fuses with life. Without such movement, meditation does not arise.

We have to understand whether the meditative way of life is excluded from other ways of life—whether it is one way provided for us, or an all-inclusive way of living. We may think that the meditative way of life is one thing and that we have to find other ways of living, making it difficult to fulfil these different ways. The Buddha said that if one practised just one of his teachings, his whole teaching would be practised. Which one was he referring to? *The teaching of awareness.* It is the only thing which embraces his whole teaching. When you are fully aware, there is no more to do. Everything will be lived fully, with all our actions, the creative movements of the present in which there is no crisis. Why are there crises in life? Because we do not live life fully, but leave a gap in which a crisis can arise.

The meditative way of life is all-inclusive, in which there is no separation or division. It is the way of harmony, communion and integration. Normally we think of the holy life being different from the life of the ordinary man. It is thought that the holy life should be left to the recluse, the mystic, and that the ordinary

45

life is for the people in the street, the 'householders'. This way of thinking is in accordance with tradition. The division between ordinary and holy has been traditional for a long time, and many of us cannot break away from this. We are afraid of a new approach and of living life fully. Out of ignorance, fear arises.

Why do we keep to tradition? It is because the mind wants security. Without security, the mind will feel there is a problem. When the mind can live with its conditions, it feels secure because it is familiar with these. This is why it attaches itself to them and tries to keep them, even when it is given the opportunity to detach. This hinders our freedom to unite within society. We may unite in certain issues, but this is not true unity. It is partial, and usually for a particular purpose, to defend our interests. Perhaps this involves opposing or killing other sections of humanity, as in the case of war, so that unity in one sector can intensify division in another sector. Individual attachment to attitudes and ideologies become group attachment and do not form the basis of true harmony in the world, because they remain self-defensive.

The meditative way of life does not mean a holy life which is 'up there'. It is simplicity in life. If we *try* to be holy, our energy is distracted to the idea of holiness, and an image of holiness is created and conformed to by dressing in a certain way, and other special forms of behaviour in order to attract attention and admiration from other people. Holiness cannot depend upon forms of beliefs. The mind creates great barriers to understanding what holiness is, because it involves us in its images. But if we look properly, we can see how false it is.

How do we really come to holiness? First of all, we have to give up any image of our holiness and penetrate to what holiness means. Can you see it? It is purity of heart, silence of mind, the movement of life whose essence is simplicity and clarity. The movement of life is truly holy—its way of moving does not disturb anything. I am not speaking of the events of life, but of life itself, which moves smoothly and evenly. Because our minds are closed to the meaning of holiness, we cannot see the movement of life.

Maybe we mostly see the dead side of life, because in the process of life we experience both life and death. When we look at the dead side of life we may feel empty, dry, and depressed. Our fear prevents us from seeing the holiness in everything, the life within death, the quality in what is ordinary. The ordinary is not something on a lower level—it means simplicity in living, thinking and feeling. There is no distinction between the holy and the ordinary. There is no need, therefore, to have the holy life institutionalised. All of us can become holy. There is no doubt that this is possible, because each of us has the capacity for enlightenment.

In Buddhism we have the word *sangha*, which has two meanings. The first is the conventional *sangha*, meaning the community of monks. The second means the one who has reached enlightenment, who has entered the Stream of Nirvana. That is the real *sangha*, which is not confined to monks but to all those who enter the Path and achieve enlightenment. Anyone of you can do this at any time, and will then take refuge in yourself, and not in a community of monks. This is the thing we are going to promote in our meditative way of life. People may say that in some cases we have to rely upon forms—we need someone to help us. But if we rely upon such help, we shall not get any practice in doing the work for ourselves and will tend to get stuck. It is like a log being carried downstream, which may get caught on one or another shore, or sink in the middle, because it is dependent upon what carries it along and has no power of its own. If we allow ourselves to be carried along by the external form of life, we can lose our way. Or if we stay in such conditions for long enough, we can begin to rot within and can no longer even float. Thus we never reach the sea of liberation.

Everyone has enough intelligence for the work, if they will use it, and will practise. But the tendency to always look for something outside to guide us, or do something for us, prevents us from using our own intelligence to recognise and tread the path. Then we get confused, because instructions coming from outside usually differ and are often contradictory. If we can just be ourselves we shall see what is best for us, and will not be misled in an age of many false teachings. This is why the Buddha gave emphasis to self-reliance. If we practise awareness of what is going on within and outside of us, we shall know more about ourselves than anyone else can do. But if we never work towards understanding ourselves, self-reliance will not be possible.

Can we renounce external support sufficiently to live alone, in the inner sense? You may think this would be a ruthless, cruel way of living, but in fact renunciation is not rejection, but taking everything that comes, everything that life gives us. We become receivers, but take nothing that is not given. We are not usually prepared to just receive things—we want to act. In order to be free from what we have, we need to renounce one thing only. Can you guess what it is? It is the self.

The renunciation of the self is the foundation of the meditative way of life. It may sound a very big thing, to renounce the self, but in fact it is not so hard. The feeling of great difficulty is the creation of the mind. It appears so hard because we are attached to the self, and want to identify ourselves with something. But it is quite possible to live without identification, in fact it makes life far easier when no self stands in the way.

Renunciation of the ego not only dissolves problems and sets the mind free, but it gives rise to selfless behaviour which is the moral aspect of the meditative way of life. Negative attitudes fade away, such as dislike, envy, competition, and are replaced by love, compassion and harmony, not because the person feels he 'ought' to behave virtuously but because goodness flows spontaneously. Without seeking pleasure, life is naturally enjoyed. Who enjoys life, if there is no self? This is the mind asking questions again, creating problems! If enjoyment is there, why worry about somebody enjoying it? We tend to put a subject there because we want *personal* satisfaction, something that we think we can hold on to or accumulate. But the nature of joy is not like that; it comes and goes, and is never fixed. You will notice that the purest form of pleasure is without self, and this is why an extreme peak of painful experience can turn to pure joy. When pain intensifies, the ego feels terrible and cannot bear it. It may try to escape, or struggle, full of fear, sometimes making the body tremble. But beyond a certain point of fear and pain, the ego gives up hope and releases its grip. The self disappears, and in that moment all suffering also disappears, leaving an impersonal purity of joy.

Personal pleasure and personal pain are two sides of one coin, both disappearing when the self is abandoned. In enlightenment the illusion or image of self is no longer there, because it is not real. It is only a figment of the consciousness. Self-abandonment is the only thing that will give us true happiness, so do not be afraid of it. We cannot do it all at once, but we can gradually stop feeding the image and weaken the idea of self. As our way of living becomes more creative and relaxed, we shall find this more and more easy to do. If we accept ourselves as we are at present, we shall be able to look without rejection at our motives, our weaknesses, our whole situation. When we criticise others, or life, we have to look into ourselves. In this way we can develop objectivity in looking, thinking and feeling. If we become more and more subjective we become more heavily identified and anxious.

Objectivity requires the capacity for aloneness. To be physically alone frequently gives rise to anxiety, which means that we cannot be mentally alone. We fill the vacuum by doing things, being with groups, or trying to become something. With some people, even the requirement to sit alone during a period of meditation presents difficulty, and this is something they can immediately practise awareness of. The apparent in-action of sitting in meditation may be the most valuable type of action. The receptive observation of what is happening in the mind and body is creative action, which will lead to enlightenment without any outside help. The only assistance that may be given is by somebody who may point out something, or an environment which is conducive to more intensive meditation for a period of time. But any teacher or guru can do nothing more than show the way. Everyone has to do his own work. We are saved by ourselves, because enlightenment lies within us.

If we follow the meditative way of life, can we still live a family life or work within society? Or would it be better to go and live 'in the forest' without house or home, wandering from place to place? No, we can live wherever we like, but we must not be bound to where or how we live. If we are enclosed by our family life we may limit ourselves. The idea of family life is not just to have a family but to learn to grow, to mature into communion with life. Married life should be a step towards psychological and emotional understanding, and the development of intuition, compassion and love. A superficial married life, in which each partner feeds the ego of the other, will merely form a hiding place, or generate negative feelings.

The Buddha said 'Good companionship is the whole of holy life', so he did not deny the value of human relationships. You may think he was referring to the companionship of monks, but this was not all he meant. He was talking of a kind of communion which can exist between people anywhere. If they have similar tendencies towards development, they can help each other by providing each other with a mirror. If you live entirely alone you may not be able to see what others see in you. It is said that the world is a mirror. This is because events often reflect your own behaviour, and also people you meet will react to you, not only because of their own personality but because of yours. People are usually more demanding than objects, and their greater sensitivity and needs require more responsibility on your part. They can make you suffer, and thus show you things about yourself that may not be noticed on your own.

Unless we are shown what we are like, we may remain ignorant and continue to blind ourselves to what is there. Good companionship with someone different from us is therefore very valuable, and this may be especially so with someone of the opposite sex. Men and women have different qualities, different strengths or weaknesses, and they can greatly help each other towards understanding. You may say that in the end we have to give up sex, and that if we get married we shall not be able to avoid it. But it is not a matter of avoiding sex, it is a matter of understanding *why* we need it. Sex is a physical and psychological need for most people, and we have to see why. Has it become a habit? Do we use it to fill an emptiness we feel? When we understand the game we are playing we shall see what it really is. Sex is not something low. All human beings are born through sex, and without it we should not be here. Feelings of guilt about sex make people anxious and neurotic, and instead of developing a more mature emotional attitude they build up a non-spiritual concept of sex.

Is there a spiritual side to sex? There is a spiritual side to everything, everywhere. As I said before, holiness is in the ordinary life. There is a spiritual side to sexuality in the surrender of self, the feeling of communion. At the highest point of sexuality, the concept of man and woman does not exist. There is complete integration, and perhaps at that moment two people can feel the movement of life in the universe. They may feel they *are* the universe, because there is no separation and there is the complete abandonment of self. However, if this is practised purely from habit, ignorance, desire, or the search for pleasure, its real meaning is lost. There is also the fear of sex, often caused by parents who will not talk about it. We have to be clear, and understand that these things are within us, otherwise we shall be further away from reality.

It is true that in the end we need to give up sex, but this celibacy cannot arise through conformity to rules or conventions. These may suppress sexuality, but do not bring about true celibacy. The desire for sex remains, and may become channelled into other drives, such as the desire for power. This can be dangerous, because the development of power without insight can destroy mankind. Celibacy only comes to be when there is understanding. Even a husband and wife can give it up naturally, without desire for it, yet can remain sleeping in one bed. We have to move towards this, but not with any feeling of compulsion to give it up— otherwise you will say 'Oh, I can't give it up!' Don't have such ideas, but that is the point we can come to. It happens naturally.

VI

WHAT BUDDHISM HAS TO OFFER TO THE WEST

WE CAN SEE that Buddhism is becoming more and more popular in the West, and we may all feel that the world today needs Buddhism. This does not mean that Buddhism should claim the monopoly for the development of spiritual life, but we can say that it can play a very important role in this field. If we believe that only Buddhism can help the world, we may become religiously neurotic, especially if we are narrow-minded and sectarian. This is because the mind is closed to other ideas and influences, and does not flow in harmony with what is actually happening in life.

It is not easy to maintain a free and balanced attitude of mind in a world which continually tends to polarise into extremes, or presents a multitude of changes and distractions to which we cannot adjust ourselves. So we go further and further outwards, looking for everything externally or relying upon opinions and ideas about the truth, instead of looking inwards to see what we are. I use the word 'we' to refer to all human beings. We cannot escape from human relationships in order to be happy. You may say that everyone has to help himself in order to get tranquillity and happiness in life. That is true, but as human beings living in society we cannot work in isolation. Certain periods of conscious withdrawal are important for intensive meditation, but of equal importance is to receive what life is giving us every moment, and to see our reactions to this. One of the main forces in life is the impact upon us of other people, and our responsibilities towards them. They can often see us in a more objective way than we can see ourselves, and make demands upon us that we should not do by ourselves. We cannot understand or deal with our own problems if we are divorced from the problems of others.

The Buddha does not deny human relationships.

Although he left his own society for a period, this did not mean that he escaped into a personal search for truth and neglected society. It is necessary for everyone to discover something profound, which usually requires a time of withdrawal from society, from the world of noise and distractions, into an environment of external silence where internal silence may be experienced, with the discovery of something new. Periods of contemplation are especially required in the modern world, whose pressures appear to leave no time for the discovery of truth, but the temporary renunciation of the external world does not mean the renunciation of human society. During most of our life, our noisy and distracting inner and outer world is the environment for developing the spiritual life.

All religions teach that contemplation is an essential part of spiritual growth and maturity, but they also teach the hard way of development through selfless action, or meditation under the stresses of daily life, without looking for reward, influence, or even results. This puts our progress to the test, revealing our weaknesses and leaving less possibility of illusion about ourselves. We are also shown the need for patience—the achievement of understanding takes time and persistence.

If we look at the world, whether Western or Eastern, we can see many forms of suffering in people. Buddhism emphasises this problem, because if we can solve it, all our striving can cease. However, the problem is not a superficial one—it is as wide and deep as life itself. The subject of suffering is often regarded as a pessimistic one, but it is a universal fact. Why do we not wish to talk about it? And why do we feel that it is pessimistic? If you look deeply into yourself, you will encounter fear—the fear of meeting life, of everything it brings or might bring to make us suffer. We want to suppress this, or leave it aside, escaping in the direction of relief or enjoyment and deluding ourselves that we are free from suffering.

Fear is the twin problem to suffering, and is deeply rooted in the mind. All of us are afraid of ourselves, and especially of our negative feelings, which we attempt to repress. We also cannot tolerate what we see as negative in other people, or in our environment, and our rejection often takes the form of aggression which conceals our underlying unhappiness. Supposing I look at someone who is miserable, or heavily serious, I may feel depressed because fear is working unconsciously in me. If we are not afraid, we shall be able to look at everything with equanimity, leaving our minds free to look into what is causing suffering. When you are nervous, instead of making efforts not to be nervous look at the nervousness itself. Look at what is really going on, and do not drive yourself to overcome it, to get rid of it, distracting your energy away from what is happening in the present. Anxiety about a fact leads us away from the fact itself.

Buddhism teaches that we should direct our attention to what is going on *now*, within us and outside us. Do not be afraid of it; do not indulge in ideas about it—just look attentively. This does not mean tensely. What is tension? It may be observed physically, but it emanates from the mind which has fear. Every time we observe unnecessary tension we can see it as a signal of anxiety, at some level or another, generated by the mind either by habit or in response to the stresses of the environment.

The mind cannot be alone; it is driven by the need for attachment, and while it remains ignorant of the truth it is continually swayed by its interests, habits, desires and sufferings. It gets caught up in the problems it has created, thus escaping from itself and pulling us into its games in order to maintain its own hold. But our work is to look at that mind, that conditioned mind, to go into it and understand it fully. By understanding how it creates problems we shall be able to see the root of suffering in ourselves and others.

Physical tensions cannot last long if the mind does not interfere. Suppose you have some bodily discomfort, if you look at it simply with the intention to see it you will notice that it changes in character. Instead of our being emotionally involved with the discomfort as a problem, we become simply aware of it as a fact. Without our wishing to overcome it, we lose our fear of it and the core of the problem drops away, leaving us lighter and clearer.

Buddhism has always emphasised the individual. It is through the change in individuals that we can have a true Alternative Society, which is of such interest to-day, especially among the young. How can we work towards an Alternative Society? First of all we must look into our present society to see whether everything in it is wrong, or whether there is any good in it. What is wrong objectively, existing in society without any connection with ourselves. Or are we individually helping to sustain or create what is wrong? Who creates society, and who will put it right? Individuals. Each one of us. We cannot separate ourselves from society, from the network of human relationships and institutions here on earth. If we want an Alternative Society we have to look to ourselves and change ourselves; change our ways of thinking, feeling, acting, and then the structures in society will spontaneously be changed.

You may say that much harm is done by present social structures, institutions and systems, and this may be true, but if they are forced away by external pressures, such as revolution, they will re-emerge in different guise as long as the source of individual egoism remains to sustain them. This permeates the entire fabric of society, and individuals tend to escape from changing themselves by directing all their attention towards changing society.

We have to look at our relationships, the basis of human society. How do we relate to other people? What is our aim? Do we have relationships because we wish to identify ourselves with others? Do we relate on a basis of desire, hatred, greed, satisfaction? Usually we want something in return when we relate to people, and become frustrated, hurt or disappointed when we do not get the appreciation or understanding we are seeking. Then we blame our situation. Are we right to do so? It is possible to relate to others without any desire for anything. You may ask what would be the point of a relationship like this.

We always look for the point, look for a reward of some kind, or for reasons. This is why there is so much argument, on the subject of self for instance. What is the point, if there is no self, of living life—there is nothing to be gained. (Gain is a basic factor in the structure of our society, because it is in the structure of ourselves.) The question of self causes confusion and contradiction. I wish to be myself, alone and free—but what is the meaning of being myself, if there is no self to be? In fact, when we say 'I am myself' we do not mean that, because 'myself' is really separate from 'I am'. I am being, not *a* being, but our language always requires subject and object, so we cannot say what the truth is. Words mislead us. This is why linguistic analysis has played such a major part in the work of Western philosophers. Yet the exploration of language has led to whole books, more and more words, on the assumption that the clarification of language will lead in the direction of truth, irrespective of the level of insight of the reader or writer. This is a very superficial approach, and it is not surprising that such literature becomes too highly complex for most people to read. The compulsive elucidation of verbal symbols distracts the mind from the work of awareness. Information, however high-powered, is not transformative.

It is true that we need words in order to communicate, but we should not overlook communication through silence. We are afraid of silence, especially when looking at each other, which makes us feel uneasy. This is because of fear, which is usually masked by conversation and movement. Words as symbols should be allowed to lead us away from their superficial aspect into the deeper significance lying behind human language. Instead of intellectual investigations, leave words alone to fulfil their practical use with as much simplicity as possible. If we are tied to certain verbal formulations, we shall find it difficult to understand other people's points of view or psychological processes. It is not a question of intelligence, but of holding to ideas expressed in specific ways, or interpreting what others say according to the face value of their words. There is therefore no freedom to listen or discuss with an open mind, which causes a kind of insensitivity and stupidity.

If you are quiet within, you will notice energy arising which will give you the stamina to continually receive what others are saying without having to impose your own opinions. We have all observed that external noise can be distracting, and can see that the *internal* noise of our ideas and impulses distracts our attention to an even greater degree. This disturbance is continuous within the personality. We may feel emotionally upset when life appears very painful and we become pre-occupied with our own problems. In an extreme state of personality disorder, it may become impossible to receive anything from others at all.

What can we do about personality disturbance? First of all—what is personality? In order to deal with the problem, we should try to understand it, otherwise our efforts to overcome it may result in further repression. Personality is like a mask, giving us an identity which we mistake for our true being, and which we hope is likeable. If people criticise or reject one of our personality traits, we feel personally hurt because we have identified ourselves with our personality. Why do we carry this mask around upon us? On the occasions when you can temporarily take it off, you will feel lighter and more free, but it is no use trying to tear it off. It will drop off gradually as we see that it is not necessary, in fact is a hindrance, to natural and spontaneous relationships, communication' and ways of living. We shall uncover what is covered, little by little, gaining freedom from illusion and disturbance. When the mask is lowered, the fundamental defence mechanisms become weaker and expose the person to a greater influence of reality. At first this involves suffering, but it is creative, not blind suffering.

Buddhism therefore understands the importance of suffering, not only as an observable fact of life but also as the means for freedom. Two of the Four Noble

Truths are the problem of suffering, and the cessation of it. The average person's first impulse, when confronted by suffering, is to put a stop to it, to overcome it, without looking to see *what* is suffering. Why not allow the ego to suffer? If we are not afraid of letting the ego suffer, we shall find our masks will burn away. Our work is to let it happen, steering a middle path between pushing ourselves too hard or running away. If we try to suppress the ego, or deal with it violently, or give it pleasure, we shall never overcome the problem of suffering.

You may notice that at a peak of psychological or physical suffering, the ego realises it cannot escape and becomes helpless, and in that moment of no hope we are free—we understand that no harm can come to us. However, if such moments of suffering come to those who refuse to let go of hope, and whose hope lies in escape, they will turn in flight and become further conditioned to fear. If the mind is not able to look at suffering, it will go on suffering.

In life there is pleasure, happiness, excitement. Life gives us many positive and negative things, and the question is whether we learn from our experiences. If we want only the positive things, do we find that this in fact leads to strength and happiness, or are all the negative things working unconsciously behind our backs? Does the act of avoiding something succeed in solving the problem? Buddhism tells us that we must observe for ourselves what is happening, why we are suffering. There is no quick and easy way out, but the way is there if we will take it. Buddhism does not promise happiness, because such an aim gives us the wrong approach. What Buddhism has to offer can only be tested by personal experience, but it can be indicated in a talk like this when the listeners give their full attention with an open mind. With a speaker like the Buddha, for instance, his discourses actually led to the enlightenment of several of his followers. This does not mean that the Buddha gave them enlightenment, but because he had seen the truth for himself he was able to point it out to others.

If we are conditioned to think that we should only listen to those who are well known and popularly recognised, giving clear explanations that we accept as the truth, we shall hinder our own understanding and that of the speaker. If we simply listen, free from preconceived ideas, in order to understand our situation, our free mind will lead us to enlightenment. Problems in listening are caused by the conditioning of the mind and by the relationship between speaker and listener.

Understanding is the foundation of enlightenment, or in pali, *sammāditthi* (*sammā* = total *ditthi* = understanding). If we have complete understanding of ourselves and our situation, what then is there left to be done? Nothing. However, it is not easy to see ourselves as we are. Is this a question of human behaviour? Some people believe that human beings are nothing but a bundle of patterns based on stimulus-response, and that in order to change behaviour there must be a reconditioning process. But Buddhism is working towards the Unconditioned, and its teaching is in the opposite direction to that of further conditioning. We do not free ourselves from one set of conditions in order to be conditioned by another set which may be more powerful and deeply rooted than previously, and thus still less accessible.

What did the Buddha mean when he advised us to rely upon ourselves? We have to play an active role in solving our own problems, because we should have the most intimate access to them and to our own capacity to look at them. Other people, whether regarded as superior in wisdom to ourselves or otherwise, can help us in various ways, but they cannot do our work for us. We have to take responsibility for ourselves, without blaming or relying upon others. This does not mean that we should depend upon our ego to lead us in the right direction, otherwise we shall deepen our conditioning and strengthen the image of our identity.

You may ask what is the meaning of reliance upon ourselves if we have no identity. Try it, and you may see that self-reliance requires alone-ness, the renunciation of outside support which later includes inner support, until ego security is lost and you stand truly alone, yet sustained by the flow of intuitive insight into everything that is. This is not an entity, or identity, because intuitive insight does not belong to anyone or accumulate anywhere. It is like light, in which it is impossible for darkness to exist. Without it, our life will be lived blindly, sometimes futilely, however good our intentions may be, because we shall be relying upon false sources of guidance. Even if we change our patterns of behaviour, they will be in accordance with a mould, a different conditioning, another set of rules.

With intuitive insight, there is no problem of right action. It will flow spontaneously, and we shall not require the leadership of others. When we see ourselves clearly, we shall also be able to understand other human beings, because behind our varied personalities lie the same basic problems and potentialities. Due to our different conditioning, we may have different forms of fear and suffering but they spring from the same source. Everybody has his personal accumulation of experience, unique to himself, but deep within us the same nature is operating, with the basic forces of what are described in Buddhism as greed, hate, and illusion (the drive to acquire or retain, the drive to avoid or reject, and the condition of non-understanding). This situation is not solved by feelings of guilt or blame, but by looking at the facts and seeing how they generate suffering.

How does intuitive insight develop? Through meditation. We shall not be able to understand what Buddhism has to offer unless we practise meditation, which is the heart of the Buddha's teaching. The Buddha himself became enlightened and inspired not through the study of Buddhism, as we know, but through meditation. He did not follow any philosophy or system in order to found his teaching, but set an example of the practice of awareness. We, on the other hand, tend to accumulate knowledge about Buddhism without putting the core of the matter into practice. Without meditation, people stay at a superficial level of the teaching, enjoying intellectual understanding and the interesting ideas they get in Buddhism.

The moral teaching of Buddhism has much in common with other religions, and also with the practical morality of non-religious people in society, so it is not in this field that Buddhism offers something new to the West. It is its method of developing the enlightenment necessary for the truly moral life which distinguishes Buddhism not only from other religions but also from other forms of meditation. The short cut it offers is the hard way, not centred around bliss or power, but based upon awareness, which links it with modern psychotherapeutic groupwork emphasising the here-and-now approach.

VII

THE PROBLEM OF CONFLICT

WHAT IS HAPPENING in the world, in organisations, in various groups of people, whether political or religious, is all a problem of conflict, is it not? Man is competing against man, one party against another party; they are all fighting and seeking for power, position, prestige, and so on. So long as there is such competitive search going on in this world of ours, conflict is always present everywhere, not only in the outside world but also in the inner world of individuals. As a matter of fact, what we are, the world is. You and I together with another create the world. So the root cause of all troubles and conflict is in each one of us existing on this Earth—nowhere else. Have you ever thought why there is such ceaseless conflict in our human affairs and existence? Why do people push others aside while attempting to get to the 'top'? What is wrong with our relationships? Unless these questions are resolved, there will never be freedom from conflict in this world. The more people try to solve problems of conflict through the pursuit of so-called peace, without understanding the root cause of the trouble, the more complicated the conflict becomes.

If you are really aware of the relationship between one person and another and among groups, you will see that all forms of relationship are based in the acquisitive mind, with its ambition and greed. There is a feeling of wanting, an expectation for something in return. Through not getting what one wants, one becomes frustrated, miserable and sorrowful. Furthermore, troubles of some kind such as quarrels, insults and so on, may also come about. Consequently, one of two things may happen: either the breaking up of relationships, or their reform. In the process of reform the conflict is still going on, if not consciously then unconsciously. Instead of trust there is suspicion and tension. Probably, one reform will cause another reform to arise, and so modify the situation. For this reason there is no end to reform, no end to modification; so fundamental change cannot be achieved through mere reform. With ideas of reforming, adjusting, adapting and modifying there can come about only a kind of change within the old conditions. This is the same as the saying: 'putting new wine into old bottles', for it is no different from decorating the walls of a prison. Nevertheless, most of us prefer to live under this superficial change and therefore in a constant state of conflict. Some people may be sensitive to this kind of living, and yet they still continue to suffer when unpleasant situations occur either to themselves or to the people around them. So sensitivity born of emotional response and not of *real understanding* will everlastingly lead to suffering and frustration as well as disappointment. But real sensitivity which comes into being together with awareness and insight will be conducive to love and compassion, enabling the person concerned to approach the problem anew. Then the *change at heart* may be attained.

Before examining the question of conflict in an individual, we should try to find out the causes of conflict in groups of people working together, either for political parties or for religious organisations. Although the two have different ideals, different goals which they are hoping to achieve, nevertheless both are working for *ideals*. Now, the fact is that between the ideals and the idealists there is a gap, the gap of how to fulfil the ideals. So long as this gap is not closed, there must be some kind of conflict among the people involved, the reason being that those who work for the ideal have different opinions and therefore believe in different ways of accomplishing that very ideal. Hence it is opinion and belief that divide the people even of the same group, so as a result there come to be the 'right' side and the 'left' side. The right fights against the left and vice versa; so both sides are confused and, being confused, they look for a leader to guide them. If the leader creates more confusion they revolt against him and try to keep him away from the leadership. Thus the conflict goes on an on. There is no end to it.

What is the reason for this? The whole answer is: people do not know *what they are*. Not knowing what they are, they just strive to be somebody and to achieve something. Then there is conflict between what they really are and what they *would like* to be or *want* to do. Being ignorant of their real state of being, such people just strive and struggle for success, mundane fulfilment and goals of that nature; they are wandering and roaming about in the darkness of self-deception and delusion. That is what is happening to our fellow-men in the present world, is it not?

What about religious people? When they get together in a group or society in order to do so-called spiritual work, they may get on with one another quite well for some time, but when the work grows and flourishes, that is to say, when something good, material or spiritual, comes out of it, they start to grasp for position status, and prestige, if there is any. Then that very grasping brings about tension, suspicion and competition within that group of people or between their group and another group. So conflict arises and enslaves them to their desire, ambition, acquisitiveness, greed, envy, jealousy, and so on. Now, the ideal or beautiful goal has become merely an image used as a ladder up which they can climb for their own interests. This stupid state of affairs can be found in any organised religious group, and it is very destructive to the *real spirit* of religion. It is true to say that the religious people themselves destroy their own religions—nobody else can do so. Buddhism is no exception. So-called Buddhists are destroying their religion by their own ignorance, stupidity, ambition and the struggle for power, fame and honour. It is also true to say that where there is strife for something, there is conflict, but when the strife ceases the conflict can no longer be found. So the best way to have freedom from conflict is not to work in conformity with any idea or ideal based on some form of belief and tradition but work for the work's *own sake*, out of compassion, love and understanding born of the unbiased, purified mind.

Turning to conflict within, we find that the life of an individual is always caught up in battles, the battles of his desires, ambitions, hopes, fears, and so forth. Is it the desire for having more, possessing more and becoming more that causes the conflict in each individual? And then this conflict, whether it be conscious or unconscious, leads to unrest and chaos in society as well as in the world as a whole, does it not? In having more possessions and property, there is fear, anxiety and worry over them. The possessor is so often afraid for the safety of his possessions that he can find no time to think for himself—or in other words, to be aware of *his own being*. Lacking the knowledge of himself and being unaware of his own conditioning, he is enmeshed in the webb of conflicting elements both within and outside himself; so he is always fighting for more security, further success and more advancement. Therefore, all his concern is for the 'more'. This is the reason why conflict plays such a very active part in people's lives, regardless of whether rich or poor, powerful or powerless.

Furthermore, thinking deeply we can find within us a hundred kinds of conflict; conflict between the old patterns and the new ones; between the known and the unknown; between belief and reason; between ideals and struggles for achievement. In short, conflict between what we *are* and what we *should be*. So the real aim for all of us is to turn to ourselves to find out what is at the heart of the matter. To understand how everything is in a state of conflict is the only way to be free from and to go beyond all forms of conflict in life. Now, the problem arises: how can the truth be understood? The truth can be discovered when the mind is completely free from all its conditions. Surely, the ordinary, petty mind is heavily burdened with knowledge, information, beliefs, traditions, religious dogmas and rituals, so it cannot be free to enquire and find out the truth. Whenever such a conditioned mind is trying to see the truth, all kinds of dogmatic assertions, philosophies and accumulated knowledge come to intervene, explaining, judging and concluding the matter so that the mind is coloured, clouded, and therefore carried away from perceiving the truth. Unless we free our minds of all conditionings, we can never understand reality, which is *un*conditioned.

In conclusion, we should remember the Buddha's words: 'All conditioned things and states belong to conflict' (sabbe sankhārā dukkhā). From this statement, we cannot regard anything in life as being free from some form of condition; it is only the conditioned and the conditioning things that flow on and on in this samsaric life. Hence the whole process of life exists in conflict of one form or another. But the cure lies in another statement of the Master: 'The stilling of the conditioned states is Happiness' (sankharanam upasano sukho). In order to still all conditioned things accumulated in your minds you have to understand what you really are, and then make the best of that knowledge. When you carry on your work with love in your heart, giving the whole of your being to the work of life, you will then be free from all conflicts and so live happily as long as your life lasts.

THE DAWN HORSE PRESS
PUBLISHERS OF CLASSIC SPIRITUAL LITERATURE

☐ Please send me information about the teaching work and availability of Bubba Free John.

☐ Please send me The Dawn Horse Press Catalog of Classic Spiritual Literature.

Name: _____

Address: _____

City: _____ State: _____ Zip: _____

THE DAWN HORSE PRESS
PUBLISHERS OF CLASSIC SPIRITUAL LITERATURE

☐ Please send me information about the teaching work and availability of Bubba Free John.

☐ Please send me The Dawn Horse Press Catalog of Classic Spiritual Literature.

Name: _____

Address: _____

City: _____ State: _____ Zip: _____

THE DAWN HORSE PRESS
Department 11
P.O. Box 3680
Clearlake Highlands, CA 95422

THE DAWN HORSE PRESS
Department 11
P.O. Box 3680
Clearlake Highlands, CA 95422